Chapter 1: Introduction to the Gut-Brain Connection

Understanding the Gut-Brain Axis

The gut-brain axis refers to the intricate communication network that links the gastrointestinal system with the brain. This connection is facilitated by a variety of pathways, including neural, hormonal, and immunological routes. The vagus nerve, which runs from the brain to the abdomen, plays a pivotal role in this communication, transmitting signals that can affect both digestive processes and emotional states. Understanding this axis is crucial for recognizing how our gut health can significantly influence our mental well-being.

Research has shown that the gut microbiome, the community of microorganisms living in our intestines, plays a key role in the gut-brain axis. These microorganisms can produce neurotransmitters and other metabolites that directly impact brain function. For instance, certain gut bacteria are known to synthesize serotonin, a neurotransmitter that regulates mood. An imbalance in the gut microbiome can lead to reduced production of these essential neurotransmitters, potentially contributing to mood disorders and other mental health issues.

The relationship between gut health and mental health is bidirectional. While the state of the gut can influence the brain, psychological stress can also affect gut function. Stress can alter gut motility and increase intestinal permeability, leading to conditions such as leaky gut syndrome. This compromised barrier allows harmful substances to enter the bloodstream, triggering inflammatory responses that can further impact mental health. Understanding this feedback loop is vital for developing effective strategies for improving both gut and brain health.

Diet plays a significant role in maintaining a healthy gut-brain axis. Nutrient-rich foods, particularly those high in fiber, prebiotics, and probiotics, can foster a balanced gut microbiome. Foods such as fruits, vegetables, whole grains, and fermented products like yogurt and kimchi support the growth of beneficial bacteria. Conversely, diets high in processed foods, sugars, and unhealthy fats can disrupt the microbiome, leading to dysbiosis and associated mental health challenges. Adopting a balanced diet is a fundamental step in nurturing both gut and brain health.

Incorporating lifestyle changes that promote a healthy gut-brain axis can lead to improved mental well-being. Regular physical activity, adequate sleep, and stress management techniques such as mindfulness and meditation can enhance gut health and, in turn, support mental health. As research continues to evolve, it becomes increasingly clear that nurturing the relationship between our gut and brain is essential for overall health. By prioritizing nutrition and lifestyle choices, individuals can take proactive steps toward enhancing their mental health through the gut-brain connection.

Historical Perspectives on Gut Health

The concept of gut health has evolved significantly over the centuries, with early civilizations recognizing the importance of digestion in overall well-being. Ancient Greek and Roman physicians, such as Hippocrates and Galen, postulated that the gut was integral to human health. Hippocrates famously stated, "All disease begins in the gut," highlighting the early acknowledgment of the connection between digestive health and disease. This perspective laid the groundwork for centuries of medical thought, establishing that the health of the digestive system could impact not just physical health but also mental well-being.

During the Middle Ages, the understanding of gut health took a different turn as the focus shifted toward humoral theory, which posited that an imbalance among the body's four humors—blood, phlegm, black bile, and yellow bile—was the root cause of illness. This theory often led to misguided treatments that overlooked the importance of diet and gut function. However, the era also saw the beginnings of herbal medicine, where practitioners utilized various plants to support digestion and alleviate gastrointestinal issues, indirectly acknowledging the significance of gut health.

The advent of modern medicine in the 19th and early 20th centuries brought about a more scientific approach to understanding gut health. Researchers began to uncover the roles of microorganisms in the digestive system, leading to the establishment of the germ theory of disease. This period marked the beginning of a more systematic investigation into the gut microbiome, and by the mid-20th century, the relationship between gut bacteria and health outcomes became a topic of interest. Studies began to reveal how an imbalance in gut flora could contribute to various health problems, including gastrointestinal disorders and their possible links to mental health issues.

As the 21st century approached, the focus on gut health accelerated, paralleling advancements in technology that allowed for deeper exploration of the microbiome. The Human Microbiome Project, launched in 2007, aimed to characterize the microorganisms found in and on the human body, emphasizing the gut's role in overall health. This project illuminated the complex interactions between gut bacteria and the body, including how these microorganisms influence immune function, metabolism, and even brain health. The realization that gut health plays a crucial role in mental health began to gain traction, leading to increased interest in the gut-brain connection.

Today, the historical perspectives on gut health inform contemporary understanding and practices in nutrition and mental health. The integration of traditional dietary practices with modern scientific research highlights the importance of a balanced gut microbiome in promoting mental wellness. As adults increasingly seek holistic approaches to health, the lessons learned from history underscore the need for a comprehensive view of nutrition, emphasizing that what we consume not only affects our physical health but also our mental state and overall quality of life. The journey through time reveals an ongoing evolution in the understanding of gut health, shaping current practices and guiding future research in the intricate relationship between nutrition and mental health.

The Importance of Mental Health

Mental health is an essential aspect of overall well-being, often overlooked in discussions about physical health. It encompasses emotional, psychological, and social well-being, influencing how individuals think, feel, and act. Mental health affects how we handle stress, relate to others, and make choices. An understanding of mental health is crucial, not only for personal wellness but also for fostering healthier communities. Recognizing its importance allows individuals to seek help, prioritize self-care, and engage in practices that enhance mental resilience.

The gut-brain connection plays a significant role in mental health, as emerging research highlights the intricate relationship between gut health and emotional well-being. The gut microbiome, a complex ecosystem of microorganisms residing in the digestive tract, influences neurotransmitter production, immune responses, and even hormonal balance. This connection suggests that maintaining a healthy gut can positively impact mood and cognitive functions. Individuals who prioritize nutrition can thus play an active role in supporting their mental health through dietary choices that promote a balanced microbiome.

Nutrition is a key factor in mental health, as what we eat directly affects brain function and emotional regulation. Diets rich in omega-3 fatty acids, antioxidants, vitamins, and minerals have been linked to lower rates of depression and anxiety. Conversely, high-sugar and high-fat diets can lead to inflammation and other physiological changes that may exacerbate mental health issues. Understanding the nutritional components that contribute to mental well-being empowers individuals to make informed dietary choices that not only nourish the body but also support optimal brain health.

Mental health issues can manifest as physical symptoms, creating a cycle that complicates both mental and physical well-being. For instance, stress and anxiety can lead to gastrointestinal disturbances, which in turn affect mood and cognitive function. This cyclical relationship underscores the importance of a holistic approach to health that integrates mental well-being with physical health. By acknowledging and addressing both aspects concurrently, individuals can break this cycle, leading to improved overall health outcomes.

Prioritizing mental health is vital for achieving a balanced and fulfilling life. By understanding the gut-brain connection and recognizing the impact of nutrition on mental well-being, individuals can take proactive steps toward enhancing their emotional health. Incorporating nutrient-rich foods into daily diets can serve as a powerful tool in promoting mental resilience and improving quality of life. Ultimately, fostering a deeper awareness of mental health and its interplay with nutrition can lead to healthier individuals and communities, creating a ripple effect of well-being throughout society.

Chapter 2: The Science of the Gut

Anatomy of the Digestive System

The digestive system is a complex network of organs and glands that work in unison to break down food, absorb nutrients, and eliminate waste. It begins in the mouth, where mechanical digestion occurs through chewing, while enzymes in saliva start the chemical breakdown of carbohydrates. The food then travels down the esophagus, a muscular tube that connects the throat to the stomach, through a series of coordinated contractions known as peristalsis. This process ensures that food moves efficiently through the digestive tract.

Once the food reaches the stomach, it encounters a highly acidic environment that further aids in digestion. The stomach's muscular walls churn the food, mixing it with gastric juices containing hydrochloric acid and digestive enzymes. This combination transforms food into a semi-liquid substance called chyme. The stomach also plays a crucial role in regulating the release of chyme into the small intestine, where the majority of nutrient absorption occurs. The sphincter at the base of the stomach controls this process, ensuring that the right amount of chyme enters the small intestine at the appropriate time.

The small intestine is divided into three sections: the duodenum, jejunum, and ileum. The duodenum is the first section and is where most chemical digestion takes place. Here, bile from the liver and digestive enzymes from the pancreas are released to further break down proteins, fats, and carbohydrates. As chyme moves through the jejunum and ileum, nutrients are absorbed through the intestinal walls and into the bloodstream. The surface area of the small intestine is significantly increased by tiny, finger-like projections called villi, which facilitate the absorption of essential nutrients and minerals.

After nutrient absorption, the remaining waste products travel into the large intestine, or colon. The primary function of the large intestine is to absorb water and electrolytes from the indigestible food matter, transforming it into a more solid form. Beneficial bacteria residing in the colon play a vital role in fermenting undigested food, further aiding in the extraction of nutrients and producing essential vitamins, such as vitamin K. The large intestine also serves as a temporary storage site for waste before it is expelled from the body through the rectum and anus.

The anatomy of the digestive system is crucial for recognizing its impact on overall health, including mental health. The gut-brain connection highlights how the digestive system's function can influence mood, cognition, and emotional well-being. A well-functioning digestive system can enhance nutrient absorption, providing the brain with the necessary components to function optimally. Conversely, digestive issues can lead to nutrient deficiencies that may negatively affect mental health, illustrating the importance of a balanced diet and proper digestive health in supporting both physical and mental well-being.

The Role of Gut Microbiota

The gut microbiota, comprising trillions of microorganisms residing in the gastrointestinal tract, plays a crucial role in maintaining overall health and well-being. These microorganisms include bacteria, viruses, fungi, and archaea, which collectively influence various physiological processes. The composition and diversity of gut microbiota can significantly affect not only digestive health but also mental health, highlighting the intricate relationship between the gut and the brain. Understanding this connection is essential for adults seeking to improve their mental well-being through nutritional choices.

Research has established that gut microbiota can produce various metabolites that influence brain function. For instance, certain gut bacteria are capable of synthesizing neurotransmitters, such as serotonin and gamma-aminobutyric acid (GABA), which are vital for regulating mood and anxiety. An estimated 90% of the body's serotonin is produced in the gut, indicating that a healthy gut microbiome is essential for optimal serotonin levels. This connection suggests that dietary choices that promote a diverse and balanced gut microbiota can have a positive impact on mental health outcomes.

The gut-brain axis, a bidirectional communication system between the gut and the brain, is essential for understanding the role of gut microbiota in mental health. Signals from the gut microbiota can influence the central nervous system through various pathways, including the vagus nerve, immune system modulation, and the production of signaling molecules. Disruptions in gut microbiota, often caused by poor dietary habits, stress, or antibiotic use, can lead to dysbiosis, which has been linked to conditions such as depression and anxiety. Thus, maintaining a healthy gut microbiome is pivotal for emotional regulation and cognitive function.

Diet plays a significant role in shaping the gut microbiota. Foods rich in fiber, such as fruits, vegetables, and whole grains, serve as prebiotics that nourish beneficial gut bacteria. Fermented foods like yogurt, kimchi, and sauerkraut introduce live beneficial bacteria into the gut, further enhancing microbial diversity. Conversely, diets high in processed foods, sugars, and unhealthy fats can promote the growth of pathogenic bacteria and contribute to dysbiosis. By making informed nutritional choices, adults can cultivate a gut environment that supports mental health and resilience against mood disorders.

The role of gut microbiota in mental health is gaining recognition as a vital area of research. The intricate interplay between gut microorganisms and brain function underscores the importance of a balanced diet rich in prebiotics and probiotics. Adults seeking to improve their mental health should consider the impact of their dietary choices on gut microbiota composition. By prioritizing gut health, individuals can foster a more favorable environment for emotional well-being, ultimately enhancing their quality of life.

How Gut Health Influences Overall Health

The relationship between gut health and overall health is a growing area of interest among researchers and health professionals. The gut, often referred to as the "second brain," plays a critical role in various bodily functions, including digestion, immune response, and even mental health. A well-functioning gut contributes to the absorption of nutrients, which are essential for maintaining energy levels and preventing chronic diseases. Conversely, an imbalanced gut microbiome can lead to a host of health issues, showcasing the profound impact that gut health has on physical well-being.

One of the key factors in gut health is the composition of the gut microbiota, which consists of trillions of microorganisms that reside in the digestive tract. These microorganisms help break down food, synthesize vitamins, and fend off harmful pathogens. A diverse and balanced microbiome is associated with better health outcomes, whereas a lack of diversity can lead to dysbiosis, a condition linked to gastrointestinal disorders, obesity, and metabolic syndrome. Maintaining a healthy gut microbiome through a balanced diet rich in fiber, probiotics, and prebiotics is essential for promoting overall health and preventing disease.

The gut also plays a crucial role in the immune system. Approximately 70% of the immune system is located in the gut, where it interacts with gut bacteria to modulate immune responses. A healthy gut can enhance the body's ability to fight infections and reduce inflammation, while an unhealthy gut may contribute to autoimmune diseases and chronic inflammation. This connection highlights the importance of gut health in supporting the immune system and underscores the need for dietary strategies that promote gut integrity.

The gut-brain axis illustrates how gut health can influence mental health. The gut microbiome produces neurotransmitters and other metabolites that can affect mood and cognitive function. For instance, the majority of serotonin, a neurotransmitter linked to feelings of happiness and well-being, is produced in the gut. Research suggests that an imbalance in gut bacteria may be associated with mental health disorders such as anxiety and depression. Therefore, prioritizing gut health is not only vital for physical health but also for maintaining emotional and psychological well-being.

The influence of gut health on overall health is significant and multifaceted. From supporting digestive efficiency and immune function to affecting mental health through the gut-brain axis, the state of the gut microbiome can have far-reaching implications. Individuals can take proactive steps to enhance their gut health by adopting a nutrient-rich diet, incorporating fermented foods, and minimizing processed foods. Recognizing the essential role of the gut in overall health empowers individuals to make informed dietary choices that can lead to improved well-being.

Chapter 3: The Brain and Its Functions

Structure of the Brain

The structure of the brain is a complex and intricate network that plays a critical role in how we think, feel, and behave. The brain is composed of several key regions, each with specific functions that contribute to our overall mental health. At its core, the brain can be divided into three main parts: the cerebrum, the cerebellum, and the brainstem. Each of these regions is essential for various cognitive and physiological processes, and understanding their structure can provide insight into how nutrition impacts brain function.

The cerebrum, the largest part of the brain, is responsible for higher cognitive functions such as reasoning, problem-solving, and emotional regulation. It is divided into two hemispheres, each containing four lobes: the frontal, parietal, temporal, and occipital lobes. The frontal lobe is particularly important for executive functions, which include planning and decision-making. Nutrition plays a vital role in supporting these processes, as certain nutrients can enhance cognitive performance and emotional stability. For example, omega-3 fatty acids found in fish have been linked to improved memory and mood regulation.

The cerebellum, located at the back of the brain, is primarily responsible for coordination and balance. It processes information from the sensory systems and integrates it with motor activity, allowing for smooth and precise movements. Although the cerebellum is often associated with physical function, emerging research suggests that it also plays a role in cognitive processes. Adequate nutrition, particularly vitamins and minerals that support nerve function, is crucial for maintaining the health of this region and ensuring optimal motor and cognitive performance.

The brainstem, which connects the brain to the spinal cord, is responsible for regulating basic life functions such as breathing, heart rate, and blood pressure. It also plays a role in regulating sleep and arousal. The brainstem is critical for survival, and its proper functioning is influenced by nutrition. For instance, deficiencies in certain B vitamins can lead to neurological issues that affect the brainstem's ability to regulate these vital functions. Ensuring a balanced diet rich in essential nutrients can support the health of the brainstem and, by extension, overall mental health.

The structure of the brain highlights the importance of nutrition in maintaining its health and function. Each region of the brain is interconnected and relies on a variety of nutrients to operate effectively. A well-balanced diet that includes a range of vitamins, minerals, and fatty acids supports not only cognitive and emotional health but also the intricate networks that link these processes together. By prioritizing nutrition, individuals can foster a healthier brain, which in turn can lead to improved mental well-being and resilience against mental health disorders.

Neurotransmitters and Mental Health

Neurotransmitters are chemical messengers that play a crucial role in transmitting signals in the brain and throughout the nervous system. They are essential for regulating numerous functions, including mood, cognition, and emotional responses. Among the most well-known neurotransmitters are serotonin, dopamine, norepinephrine, and gamma-aminobutyric acid (GABA). Each of these transmitters contributes to mental health in unique ways. For instance, serotonin is often referred to as the "feel-good" neurotransmitter, as it is associated with feelings of happiness and well-being. In contrast, dopamine is linked to the brain's reward system, influencing motivation and pleasure. Understanding the balance and function of these neurotransmitters is critical for comprehending the complex relationship between nutrition and mental health.

Research indicates that the gut microbiome significantly influences the production and regulation of neurotransmitters. The gut contains a vast network of neurons, often referred to as the "second brain," which communicates with the central nervous system. Certain gut bacteria are involved in the synthesis of neurotransmitters like serotonin; in fact, approximately 90% of the body's serotonin is produced in the gut. Therefore, the health of the gut microbiome can directly impact mood and emotional health. Maintaining a diverse and balanced gut flora through proper nutrition, including the consumption of probiotics and prebiotics, can enhance neurotransmitter production and support mental well-being.

Dietary choices can have profound effects on neurotransmitter levels. For example, the amino acid tryptophan, a precursor to serotonin, is found in foods like turkey, nuts, and seeds. Consuming a diet rich in these foods can promote serotonin production, potentially alleviating symptoms of depression and anxiety. Similarly, dopamine production is influenced by the availability of tyrosine, another amino acid that can be found in protein-rich foods such as lean meats, fish, and dairy products. By prioritizing a nutrient-dense diet that supports the synthesis of key neurotransmitters, individuals can proactively manage their mental health.

The relationship between nutrition and neurotransmitter function extends to the impact of micronutrients. Vitamins and minerals such as B vitamins, magnesium, and zinc are essential for the proper functioning of neurotransmitters. For instance, deficiencies in B vitamins can lead to reduced synthesis of neurotransmitters like serotonin and dopamine, which may exacerbate mood disorders. Incorporating a variety of fruits, vegetables, whole grains, and lean proteins into one's diet can help ensure adequate intake of these vital nutrients, ultimately supporting cognitive function and emotional stability.

Neurotransmitters play a pivotal role in mental health, and their production and function are intricately linked to nutrition. A well-balanced diet that includes the right macronutrients and micronutrients can enhance neurotransmitter synthesis, positively influencing mood and mental well-being. By recognizing the significance of the gut-brain connection and making informed dietary choices, individuals can take proactive steps to support their mental health through nutrition. Emphasizing the consumption of nutrient-rich foods can empower individuals to foster a healthier mind and body, underlining the profound impact that what we eat has on our mental state.

The Impact of Stress on Brain Function

Stress is a complex physiological response that can significantly influence brain function. When the body perceives a threat, whether real or imagined, it activates the hypothalamic-pituitary-adrenal (HPA) axis, leading to the release of stress hormones like cortisol and adrenaline. While these hormones serve essential roles in survival by preparing the body for a fight-or-flight response, chronic exposure to stress can lead to detrimental changes in the brain. Over time, elevated cortisol levels can impair neuroplasticity, the brain's ability to adapt and reorganize itself, which is crucial for learning and memory.

One of the most notable effects of chronic stress is its impact on the hippocampus, a region integral to memory formation and emotional regulation. Prolonged high levels of cortisol can lead to the atrophy of hippocampal neurons, resulting in difficulties with memory recall and an increased risk of mood disorders such as depression and anxiety. Research has shown that individuals experiencing high levels of stress often report issues with concentration and decision-making, further illustrating how stress can disrupt cognitive processes. This impairment can create a vicious cycle, as difficulties in managing stress can lead to more stress, compounding the cognitive decline.

Stress can alter the communication pathways within the brain, particularly affecting neurotransmitter systems. For instance, stress has been associated with dysregulation of serotonin and dopamine, two critical neurotransmitters involved in mood regulation and pleasure. When these systems are disrupted, individuals may experience heightened feelings of anxiety or depression, further complicating mental health challenges. The interplay between stress, neurotransmitter function, and overall brain health underscores the importance of managing stress effectively to maintain optimal cognitive function.

The gut-brain connection plays a significant role in how stress affects brain function. The gut microbiome, composed of trillions of microorganisms, can influence the brain's response to stress. Stress has been shown to alter gut permeability and microbial composition, potentially leading to dysbiosis. This imbalance in gut bacteria can, in turn, affect the production of neurotransmitters and other neuroactive compounds, further exacerbating stress-related cognitive impairments. Therefore, addressing gut health through proper nutrition and lifestyle choices can be a crucial strategy for mitigating the effects of stress on brain function.

When understanding the impact of stress on brain function is vital for adults seeking to improve their mental health. Acknowledging the physiological changes that occur during chronic stress can empower individuals to adopt healthier coping mechanisms and engage in preventive strategies. By prioritizing stress management techniques, such as mindfulness, exercise, and proper nutrition, adults can protect their cognitive health and foster a more resilient brain, ultimately enhancing their overall well-being.

Chapter 4: Nutrition and Its Impact on the Gut

Essential Nutrients for Gut Health

Maintaining a healthy gut is crucial for overall well-being, as it plays a significant role in both physical and mental health. Essential nutrients are foundational to gut health, influencing the balance of gut microbiota, the integrity of the gut lining, and the ability to absorb nutrients effectively. Among these nutrients, dietary fiber, probiotics, prebiotics, healthy fats, and certain vitamins and minerals stand out as particularly beneficial for promoting a flourishing gut environment.

Dietary fiber is one of the most important components of a gut-friendly diet. It is found in fruits, vegetables, whole grains, legumes, and nuts. Fiber acts as a bulking agent, facilitating regular bowel movements and preventing constipation. Furthermore, soluble fiber can ferment in the gut, serving as food for beneficial bacteria. This fermentation process not only supports the growth of a diverse microbiome but also produces short-chain fatty acids (SCFAs), which have anti-inflammatory properties and can enhance the gut barrier function.

Probiotics are live microorganisms, often referred to as "good" bacteria, that confer health benefits when consumed in adequate amounts. They can be found in fermented foods such as yogurt, kefir, sauerkraut, and kimchi, or taken as supplements. Probiotics help maintain a balanced gut microbiota, which is vital for digestive health and immune function. They can also help alleviate symptoms of gastrointestinal disorders, such as irritable bowel syndrome (IBS) and inflammatory bowel disease (IBD). By supporting a healthy microbiome, probiotics can contribute to improved mental health as well, given the gut-brain connection.

Prebiotics, on the other hand, are non-digestible food components that serve as nourishment for probiotics. Foods rich in prebiotics include garlic, onions, leeks, asparagus, bananas, and oats. By promoting the growth and activity of beneficial gut bacteria, prebiotics enhance gut health and improve digestion. They also play a role in the production of SCFAs, which can influence brain function and mood regulation. Ensuring an adequate intake of both prebiotics and probiotics can strengthen the gut-brain axis, fostering a positive impact on mental health.

Healthy fats, particularly omega-3 fatty acids found in fatty fish, flaxseeds, and walnuts, are also essential for gut health. These fats possess anti-inflammatory properties that can help reduce gut inflammation and promote a healthy microbiome. Additionally, certain vitamins and minerals, such as vitamin D, zinc, and magnesium, are crucial for maintaining the integrity of the gut lining and supporting immune responses. A diet rich in these nutrients not only promotes gut health but also supports cognitive function and emotional well-being, highlighting the intricate relationship between nutrition and mental health.

The Role of Probiotics and Prebiotics

The role of probiotics and prebiotics in maintaining gut health has gained significant attention in recent years, particularly in relation to mental health. Probiotics are live microorganisms that, when consumed in adequate amounts, confer health benefits to the host. These beneficial bacteria help to balance the gut microbiome, which is crucial for overall health, including mental well-being. By influencing the gut-brain axis, a complex communication network linking the gut and the brain, probiotics may play a vital role in reducing symptoms of anxiety and depression, as well as enhancing cognitive function.

Prebiotics, on the other hand, are non-digestible food components that promote the growth and activity of beneficial gut bacteria. They serve as food for probiotics, helping to enhance their effectiveness.

Common sources of prebiotics include dietary fibers found in fruits, vegetables, and whole grains. By increasing the population of beneficial bacteria in the gut, prebiotics can improve digestion, boost immunity, and may even influence mood and mental health. The synergy between probiotics and prebiotics is essential, as a healthy gut microbiome is associated with improved mental health outcomes.

Research indicates that the gut microbiome can influence the production of neurotransmitters, such as serotonin, which is often referred to as the "feel-good" hormone. Approximately 90% of the body's serotonin is produced in the gut. Probiotics have been shown to enhance the availability of these neurotransmitters, potentially alleviating symptoms of depression and anxiety. This connection underscores the importance of nurturing gut health through dietary choices that include both probiotics and prebiotics.

Incorporating probiotics and prebiotics into one's diet can be achieved through various food sources. Fermented foods such as yogurt, kefir, sauerkraut, and kimchi are excellent sources of probiotics. Meanwhile, foods rich in fiber, such as bananas, asparagus, onions, and garlic, provide the necessary prebiotics to support the growth of these beneficial bacteria. Additionally, dietary supplements containing specific strains of probiotics can also be effective for individuals who may not consume enough through food alone.

The role of probiotics and prebiotics highlights the importance of a balanced diet for mental health. The interplay between the gut microbiome and the brain suggests that what we eat can significantly influence our emotional and cognitive well-being. As research in this field continues to evolve, incorporating these elements into daily nutrition may offer a simple yet powerful strategy to enhance mental health and overall quality of life.

Dietary Patterns and Their Effects

Dietary patterns significantly influence both physical and mental health, a concept that is increasingly supported by research in the field of nutrition and psychology. The foods we consume not only provide essential nutrients but also impact the gut microbiome, which plays a critical role in the gut-brain connection. Different dietary patterns, such as the Mediterranean diet, Western diet, and plant-based diets, have distinct effects on mental health outcomes. Understanding these patterns can help individuals make informed choices about their nutrition and overall well-being.

The Mediterranean diet is characterized by high consumption of fruits, vegetables, whole grains, legumes, nuts, and healthy fats, particularly olive oil. This dietary pattern has been associated with lower rates of depression and anxiety. Studies suggest that the anti-inflammatory properties of Mediterranean foods and their rich content of omega-3 fatty acids contribute to improved mood and cognitive function. Furthermore, the diet's emphasis on social eating and shared meals may enhance emotional well-being, reinforcing the connection between nutrition and mental health.

The Western diet, which is typically high in processed foods, sugar, and unhealthy fats, has been linked to adverse mental health outcomes. Research indicates that individuals who consume a Western-style diet may be at a higher risk for developing mood disorders, including depression and anxiety. The high levels of refined sugars and unhealthy fats can lead to inflammation and oxidative stress, both of which have been implicated in the development of neuropsychiatric conditions. This connection underscores the importance of dietary choices in maintaining mental health.

Plant-based diets, which prioritize whole, unprocessed plant foods, have also garnered attention for their potential benefits for mental well-being. Evidence suggests that individuals adhering to plant-based diets often report lower levels of stress and improved mood. The abundance of antioxidants, vitamins, and minerals found in fruits and vegetables may enhance brain function and reduce the risk of cognitive decline. Additionally, plant-based diets tend to be lower in saturated fats and higher in fiber, promoting a healthy gut microbiome, which is crucial for optimal brain function.

The relationship between dietary patterns and mental health is complex and multifaceted. While specific diets may offer certain advantages, the key lies in adopting a balanced and varied approach to nutrition. Incorporating a range of nutrient-dense foods can support both gut and brain health, leading to improved mental health outcomes. As research continues to evolve, it is essential for individuals to consider how their dietary choices can impact their overall mental well-being and to seek guidance from healthcare professionals when making significant changes to their nutrition.

Chapter 5: Nutrition's Influence on Mental Health

Nutritional Deficiencies and Mental Disorders

Nutritional deficiencies have emerged as significant contributors to various mental disorders, highlighting the intricate relationship between diet and mental health. Deficiencies in essential nutrients such as vitamins, minerals, omega-3 fatty acids, and amino acids can adversely affect brain function and overall mental well-being. Research has demonstrated that inadequate intake of these nutrients may lead to an increased risk of conditions such as depression, anxiety, and cognitive decline. Understanding the specific nutrients involved and their roles in brain health is crucial for developing effective dietary strategies that support mental wellness.

One of the most studied nutrients in relation to mental health is omega-3 fatty acids, particularly EPA and DHA, which are crucial for maintaining neuronal structure and function. These fatty acids play a vital role in reducing inflammation and promoting neuroplasticity, the brain's ability to adapt and reorganize itself. A deficiency in omega-3s has been correlated with increased rates of depression and anxiety. Individuals who consume diets low in these essential fats may experience a decline in mood and cognitive function, underscoring the importance of incorporating sources such as fatty fish, flaxseeds, and walnuts into their diets.

Vitamins and minerals also play a pivotal role in mental health. For instance, deficiencies in B vitamins, particularly B6, B12, and folate, have been linked to an increased risk of mood disorders. These vitamins are integral to neurotransmitter synthesis and energy metabolism within the brain. Similarly, minerals like zinc and magnesium have been shown to influence brain function and emotional regulation.

A lack of these nutrients can lead to alterations in mood and cognitive processes, suggesting that a well-balanced diet rich in vitamins and minerals is essential for maintaining mental health.

Amino acids, the building blocks of proteins, are also critical in the context of mental health. Certain amino acids, like tryptophan and tyrosine, are precursors to neurotransmitters such as serotonin and dopamine, which are vital for mood regulation and cognitive function. A diet insufficient in these amino acids may disrupt the production of these neurotransmitters, potentially leading to mood disorders and cognitive impairments. Ensuring adequate protein intake from a variety of sources can help mitigate these risks and support optimal mental health.

Addressing nutritional deficiencies requires a comprehensive approach that includes dietary modifications, supplementation when necessary, and ongoing education about the importance of nutrition for mental health. Health professionals and individuals alike must prioritize a nutrient-dense diet that supports brain function and emotional well-being. By recognizing the link between nutrition and mental disorders, individuals can take proactive steps to enhance their mental health through informed dietary choices, ultimately fostering a healthier relationship between the gut and the brain.

The Link Between Inflammation and Mental Health

Chronic inflammation has emerged as a critical factor influencing various aspects of health, including mental health. Research indicates that inflammation can affect brain function and behavior, contributing to the development and exacerbation of mental health disorders such as depression and anxiety. The brain's immune system, which includes microglia and other immune cells, can become activated in response to inflammatory signals. This activation can lead to neuroinflammation, disrupting neurotransmitter production and signaling pathways essential for mood regulation.

The gut microbiome plays a pivotal role in modulating inflammation throughout the body, including the brain. A balanced gut microbiome contributes to the production of short-chain fatty acids, which possess anti-inflammatory properties. When the gut is compromised, either through a poor diet, antibiotics, or other factors, it can lead to dysbiosis, an imbalance in gut bacteria. This dysbiosis can trigger systemic inflammation, which may spill over into the central nervous system and influence mental health outcomes. Therefore, maintaining gut health is crucial for managing inflammation and promoting mental well-being.

Dietary choices significantly impact both gut health and inflammation levels. Foods rich in antioxidants, omega-3 fatty acids, and fiber can help reduce inflammation and support a healthy gut microbiome. Conversely, diets high in processed foods, sugars, and unhealthy fats are associated with increased inflammation. By adopting an anti-inflammatory diet, individuals can potentially lower their risk of developing mental health issues. Incorporating whole foods such as fruits, vegetables, whole grains, lean proteins, and healthy fats can foster a nourishing environment for both the gut and the brain.

The relationship between inflammation and mental health is bidirectional. Not only can inflammation contribute to mental health disorders, but mental health conditions can also lead to increased inflammation. Stress, for instance, is known to activate the body's inflammatory response, creating a vicious cycle that can be difficult to break. Individuals experiencing chronic stress or mental health issues may benefit from interventions aimed at reducing inflammation, such as mindfulness practices, regular exercise, and dietary modifications.

The link between inflammation and mental health underscores the importance of a holistic approach to well-being. By prioritizing gut health through nutrition and lifestyle choices, individuals can potentially mitigate the inflammatory processes that contribute to mental health disorders.
Recognizing the interconnectedness of the gut and brain empowers

individuals to make informed choices that support their mental health, emphasizing that nutrition is a powerful tool in the quest for emotional balance and resilience.

Foods That Boost Mood and Cognitive Function

The relationship between nutrition and mental health is increasingly recognized, with specific foods shown to enhance mood and cognitive function. A well-balanced diet rich in certain nutrients can support brain health, improve emotional well-being, and even combat cognitive decline. Understanding which foods to incorporate into your daily meals can empower you to make choices that positively influence your mental state.

Fatty fish, such as salmon, mackerel, and sardines, are excellent sources of omega-3 fatty acids, which play a crucial role in brain health. These essential fats are known to reduce inflammation and promote neurogenesis, the process of forming new neurons. Research suggests that regular consumption of omega-3s can lead to improved mood and a lower risk of depression. Incorporating fatty fish into your diet a few times a week can provide these beneficial effects, supporting both cognitive function and emotional stability.

Another group of foods that contribute to mental well-being is fruits and vegetables, particularly those rich in antioxidants. Berries, leafy greens, and cruciferous vegetables are packed with vitamins and minerals that protect the brain from oxidative stress, a factor linked to cognitive decline. Antioxidants help neutralize free radicals, which can damage brain cells. Including a variety of colorful fruits and vegetables in your meals not only enhances your overall nutrition but also specifically targets brain health, promoting a clearer mind and better mood.

Whole grains, such as oats, brown rice, and quinoa, are integral to maintaining stable blood sugar levels, which is vital for consistent energy and mood regulation. These complex carbohydrates are digested slowly, preventing spikes and crashes in blood sugar that can lead to irritability and fatigue. Additionally, whole grains are rich in fiber, which supports gut health—a key player in the gut-brain connection. A balanced diet that incorporates whole grains can thus foster both physical health and mental clarity.

Fermented foods like yogurt, kefir, and sauerkraut are gaining attention for their role in enhancing gut health, which is intricately linked to mental well-being. These foods contain probiotics that promote a healthy microbiome, which in turn can influence neurotransmitter production in the brain. Various studies have indicated that a healthy gut can lead to improved mood and cognitive function, as well as a reduced risk of anxiety and depression. Including fermented foods in your diet can be an effective strategy for supporting both gut and brain health, creating a holistic approach to mental wellness.

Chapter 6: The Role of Fiber in Gut and Brain Health

Types of Dietary Fiber

Dietary fiber is an essential component of a balanced diet, playing a significant role in both digestive health and overall well-being. There are two primary types of dietary fiber: soluble and insoluble, each with distinct characteristics and health benefits. Understanding these types can empower individuals to make informed dietary choices that not only support gut health but also enhance mental well-being.

Soluble fiber dissolves in water, forming a gel-like substance in the digestive tract. This type of fiber is found in foods such as oats, beans, lentils, apples, and citrus fruits. Soluble fiber is known for its ability to help regulate blood sugar levels by slowing the absorption of glucose. This can be particularly beneficial for individuals managing conditions such as diabetes. Additionally, soluble fiber is effective in lowering cholesterol levels, which may contribute to improved heart health. The fermentation of soluble fiber by gut bacteria also produces short-chain fatty acids, which have been linked to various mental health benefits, including reduced symptoms of anxiety and depression.

Insoluble fiber does not dissolve in water and adds bulk to the digestive system, aiding in regular bowel movements. It is primarily found in whole grains, nuts, seeds, and the skins of fruits and vegetables. This type of fiber is crucial for maintaining digestive health by promoting regularity and preventing constipation. Furthermore, insoluble fiber may help reduce the risk of developing diverticular disease and other gastrointestinal disorders. Its role in fostering a healthy gut environment is particularly significant, as a well-functioning gut is increasingly recognized for its connection to mental health.

Both types of dietary fiber are vital for a healthy diet, and they often work best in combination. A diet rich in a variety of fiber sources can support the diverse community of gut bacteria, known as the microbiome. A healthy microbiome is essential for not only digestive health but also for the production of neurotransmitters and other compounds that influence mood and cognitive function. Research suggests that an imbalance in gut bacteria may be linked to conditions such as depression and anxiety, highlighting the importance of fiber in fostering a balanced gut environment.

Incorporating an array of fiber-rich foods into the diet can promote both physical and mental health. Adults should aim for at least 25 to 30 grams of dietary fiber each day, focusing on whole, unprocessed foods to maximize the benefits. By understanding the types of dietary fiber and their respective roles, individuals can make dietary choices that support their gut health, enhance their well-being, and ultimately contribute to a healthier mind. Balancing soluble and insoluble fiber intake can be a simple yet effective strategy for improving overall health and nurturing the gut-brain connection.

Fiber's Impact on Gut Microbiota

Fiber plays a crucial role in shaping the composition and function of gut microbiota, the complex community of microorganisms residing in our intestines. These microorganisms, including bacteria, fungi, and viruses, significantly influence our health, particularly our mental health, by producing metabolites that affect brain function and mood regulation. A diet rich in fiber supports the growth of beneficial bacteria, which in turn leads to improved gut health and potentially enhances cognitive functions. Understanding the interplay between fiber and gut microbiota can provide insights into how dietary choices directly influence mental well-being.

Different types of dietary fiber, such as soluble and insoluble fiber, have distinct effects on gut microbiota. Soluble fiber, found in foods like oats, legumes, and fruits, dissolves in water to form a gel-like substance in the gut. This type of fiber is fermentable, meaning it can be broken down by gut bacteria, producing short-chain fatty acids (SCFAs) that have anti-inflammatory properties and serve as an energy source for colon cells. In contrast, insoluble fiber, found in whole grains and vegetables, adds bulk to stool and aids in regular bowel movements. Both types of fiber contribute to a healthy microbiome, but their specific effects can vary, emphasizing the importance of a diverse fiber intake.

The fermentation of fiber by gut bacteria leads to the production of SCFAs, which play a vital role in the gut-brain axis. These fatty acids not only nourish the cells of the colon but also enter the bloodstream and can influence brain function. Research has shown that SCFAs can modulate neurotransmitter production, reduce inflammation, and even alter gene expression related to brain health. A well-balanced diet that includes a variety of fiber sources can therefore foster a microbiome that supports the production of these beneficial metabolites, promoting mental clarity and emotional stability.

The diversity of gut microbiota is crucial for maintaining mental health. A higher diversity of gut bacteria is associated with lower levels of anxiety and depression. Fiber-rich diets have been shown to increase microbial diversity by providing the necessary nutrients that different bacterial species require to thrive. This diversity not only enhances the resilience of the gut microbiome but also ensures a more robust production of metabolites that support cognitive function. Consequently, individuals who consume a diet high in fiber are likely to experience better mood regulation and reduced symptoms of mental health disorders.

Incorporating a wide range of fiber-rich foods into the diet is essential for supporting gut microbiota and, by extension, mental health. Whole grains, fruits, vegetables, legumes, nuts, and seeds are all excellent sources of dietary fiber. Transitioning to a fiber-rich diet may require gradual changes to avoid gastrointestinal discomfort, particularly for those who are not accustomed to high fiber intake. However, the long-term benefits of improved gut health and enhanced mental well-being make the effort worthwhile. By prioritizing fiber in our diets, we can cultivate a healthier gut microbiome, ultimately fostering a stronger connection between our gut and our brain.

Fiber-Rich Foods for Mental Clarity

Fiber-rich foods play a crucial role in maintaining mental clarity, largely due to their impact on gut health. Research has established a strong connection between the gut microbiome and cognitive function, suggesting that the types of foods we consume can significantly influence our mental well-being. Fiber acts as a prebiotic, providing nourishment for beneficial gut bacteria. When these bacteria thrive, they produce short-chain fatty acids and other metabolites that support brain health, reducing inflammation and enhancing cognitive processes.

Whole grains, legumes, fruits, and vegetables are excellent sources of dietary fiber. Incorporating foods such as oats, quinoa, lentils, apples, and broccoli into your daily meals can promote a healthy gut microbiome. For instance, oats contain beta-glucans, a type of soluble fiber that not only aids digestion but also has been linked to improved mood and cognitive function. Similarly, legumes like chickpeas and black beans offer substantial fiber while also being rich in protein, making them an excellent choice for maintaining energy levels and mental acuity throughout the day.

In addition to whole foods, fermented fiber-rich products can further enhance gut health and mental clarity. Foods such as yogurt, kefir, sauerkraut, and kimchi not only provide fiber but also introduce beneficial probiotics into the digestive system. Probiotics are known to interact with the gut-brain axis, influencing neurotransmitter production and potentially alleviating symptoms of anxiety and depression. The synergy between fiber and probiotics creates an environment conducive to optimal brain function, making these foods a vital part of a balanced diet.

The consumption of fiber-rich foods can help stabilize blood sugar levels, which is essential for maintaining focus and energy. Fluctuations in blood sugar can lead to mood swings, irritability, and decreased cognitive performance. By choosing high-fiber foods that digest slowly, individuals can experience more consistent energy levels, allowing for improved concentration and mental clarity. This stability is particularly important in today's fast-paced world, where the ability to think clearly and respond effectively is paramount.

It is essential to approach dietary changes gradually to maximize the benefits of fiber-rich foods. Increasing fiber intake too quickly can lead to digestive discomfort, so it is advisable to incorporate these foods into your diet slowly. Additionally, staying hydrated is crucial, as fiber works best when combined with adequate fluid intake. By thoughtfully integrating fiber-rich foods into your meals, adults can enhance their gut health and, consequently, their mental clarity, paving the way for improved overall mental well-being.

Chapter 7: The Effects of Sugar and Processed Foods

Sugar's Impact on Mood and Behavior

Research indicates that sugar consumption can significantly affect mood and behavior, leading to a complex interplay between dietary habits and mental health. Sugar, particularly in the form of refined carbohydrates and added sugars, can cause rapid fluctuations in blood glucose levels. These spikes and subsequent crashes can result in feelings of irritability, fatigue, and anxiety. The body's response to these changes can lead to a cycle where individuals may seek additional sugary foods to regain a sense of energy and well-being, perpetuating the mood swings associated with sugar consumption.

The neurobiological mechanisms underlying sugar's impact on mood involve the release of neurotransmitters, particularly dopamine. When sugar is consumed, the brain's reward system is activated, leading to a temporary boost in mood and feelings of pleasure. This biochemical response can create a sense of dependency, similar to addictive substances, where individuals seek sugar to replicate the pleasurable feelings. Over time, however, the repeated consumption of sugar can desensitize the brain's reward pathways, leading to diminished feelings of satisfaction and increased cravings, which can exacerbate mood disorders.

Its direct effects on the brain, sugar can also influence gut health, which further impacts mood and behavior. The gut microbiome plays a critical role in the production of neurotransmitters, including serotonin, which is often referred to as the "feel-good" hormone. High sugar intake can lead to dysbiosis, an imbalance in gut bacteria that can negatively affect mental health. A disrupted microbiome may lead to increased inflammation and a higher risk of anxiety and depression, highlighting the importance of a balanced diet in maintaining both gut health and emotional well-being.

The societal and psychological factors surrounding sugar consumption cannot be overlooked. Many individuals associate sugary foods with comfort and reward, often consuming them during times of stress or emotional distress. This behavior can create a feedback loop where emotional eating becomes a coping mechanism, reinforcing negative patterns and contributing to poor mental health outcomes. Addressing these behaviors requires a multifaceted approach, including mindful eating practices and the development of healthier coping strategies that do not rely on sugar for emotional relief.

The impact of sugar on mood and behavior is crucial for adults seeking to improve their overall mental health. By recognizing the signs of sugar-related mood fluctuations and their connection to dietary choices, individuals can make informed decisions about their nutrition. Reducing sugar intake and focusing on a balanced diet rich in whole foods may not only support physical health but also foster emotional resilience, creating a more stable foundation for mental well-being in the long run.

The Dangers of Processed Foods

Processed foods have become a staple in many diets, primarily due to their convenience and widespread availability. However, these foods often come with a range of health risks that can adversely affect both physical health and mental well-being. The term "processed food" encompasses a broad category, including items that have been altered through methods such as canning, freezing, or addition of preservatives and artificial ingredients. While not all processed foods are detrimental, many are stripped of essential nutrients and contain high levels of sugar, salt, and unhealthy fats, which can lead to various health issues.

One significant concern regarding processed foods is their impact on gut health. The gut microbiome, a complex community of microorganisms in the digestive tract, plays a crucial role in overall health, including mental health. Diets high in processed foods can disrupt the balance of this microbiome, leading to dysbiosis, which is associated with conditions like anxiety and depression. Studies have shown that a diet rich in whole foods, such as fruits, vegetables, and whole grains, supports a healthier gut microbiome, while processed foods can foster the growth of harmful bacteria, exacerbating mental health issues.

Processed foods often contain additives and preservatives that may have negative effects on cognitive function. Ingredients such as artificial sweeteners, flavor enhancers, and colorings have been linked to various health concerns, including hyperactivity in children and cognitive decline in adults. These substances can interfere with neurotransmitter balance and brain function, potentially leading to mood disorders and cognitive impairments. The consumption of such additives in excessive amounts can create a cycle of dependency, as individuals may seek out these foods for their immediate gratification, unaware of the long-term consequences on their mental health.

The high sugar content in many processed foods can lead to significant fluctuations in blood sugar levels, which can affect mood and energy levels. The rapid rise and fall of blood sugar can result in irritability, anxiety, and fatigue, further complicating mental health issues. Over time, excessive sugar intake can contribute to inflammation and oxidative stress, both of which are implicated in the development of chronic diseases and mental health disorders. This underscores the importance of being mindful of sugar consumption, particularly from processed sources.

The dangers of processed foods extend beyond physical health and have profound implications for mental well-being. As research continues to illuminate the gut-brain connection, it becomes increasingly clear that dietary choices play a pivotal role in shaping not only our physical health but also our mental state. By prioritizing whole, minimally processed foods, individuals can foster a healthier gut microbiome, stabilize mood, and enhance overall mental health. Making informed dietary choices is a vital step towards achieving better health outcomes and improving quality of life.

Strategies for Reducing Sugar Intake

Reducing sugar intake is essential for improving overall health and supporting mental well-being. One effective strategy is to become more aware of hidden sugars in everyday foods. Many processed items, such as sauces, bread, and salad dressings, contain added sugars that can easily go unnoticed. Reading nutrition labels carefully can help consumers identify these hidden sugars. By recognizing how much sugar is present in various foods, individuals can make more informed choices and gradually reduce their overall sugar consumption.

Another important strategy is to replace sugary snacks with healthier alternatives. Instead of reaching for candy or pastries, adults can opt for fruits, nuts, or yogurt as satisfying snacks. These alternatives not only provide essential nutrients but also deliver natural sweetness without the added sugars found in many processed options. Preparing snacks in advance can make it easier to resist the temptation of sugary treats when hunger strikes. This simple shift can significantly lower sugar intake while promoting healthier eating habits.

Incorporating more whole foods into meals is also a powerful way to reduce sugar consumption. Whole foods, such as vegetables, whole grains, and lean proteins, tend to be lower in sugar and higher in fiber. Increasing the intake of these foods can help stabilize blood sugar levels, which is crucial for maintaining energy and reducing cravings for sugary foods. Planning balanced meals that prioritize whole ingredients can improve physical health and positively influence mental health by alleviating mood swings and irritability associated with sugar fluctuations.

Mindful eating practices can further support efforts to cut back on sugar. By paying attention to hunger cues and savoring each bite, individuals can develop a healthier relationship with food. This practice encourages eating more slowly and appreciating the flavors of meals, which can reduce the desire for additional sugary options.

Mindfulness techniques, such as deep breathing or meditation before meals, can also help individuals make conscious food choices rather than succumbing to impulsive eating driven by stress or boredom.

Seeking support from friends, family, or professionals can enhance the journey toward reducing sugar intake. Engaging in group activities focused on healthy eating, sharing recipes, or even participating in cooking classes can create a sense of community and accountability. Additionally, consulting with a registered dietitian can provide personalized strategies and guidance tailored to individual needs. By fostering a supportive environment, adults can navigate the challenges of reducing sugar intake more effectively and sustain their commitment to better health and mental clarity.

Chapter 8: The Importance of Hydration

How Water Affects Gut Function

Water plays a pivotal role in maintaining optimal gut function, acting as a crucial element for digestion, nutrient absorption, and overall gastrointestinal health. The gut requires adequate hydration to carry out its various functions efficiently. Water is essential for the breakdown of food, as it helps in the formation of digestive juices, including saliva and gastric acid. These fluids are necessary for the enzymatic processes that break down food into absorbable nutrients, ensuring that the body receives the vitamins, minerals, and energy it needs to function effectively.

To aiding digestion, water contributes to the movement of food through the digestive tract. It helps to soften stool and prevent constipation, a common issue that can be exacerbated by inadequate fluid intake. When the body is dehydrated, the colon absorbs more water from the waste material, leading to harder stools that are difficult to pass. This not only affects comfort but can also lead to more serious digestive issues. Staying well-hydrated is therefore critical for maintaining regular bowel movements and promoting overall gut health.

The gut microbiome, which consists of trillions of microorganisms residing in the gastrointestinal tract, also relies on proper hydration. These microbes play a significant role in digestion, metabolism, and immune function. A well-hydrated environment fosters a balanced microbiome, promoting the growth of beneficial bacteria while inhibiting harmful pathogens. Research suggests that dehydration can alter the composition of gut bacteria, potentially leading to dysbiosis, which has been linked to various health issues, including inflammatory bowel disease and metabolic disorders.

Water facilitates the absorption of nutrients. Once food is broken down, the small intestine absorbs essential nutrients and water-soluble vitamins. Adequate hydration ensures that this process occurs smoothly, allowing for the efficient transportation of nutrients into the bloodstream. Conversely, dehydration can hinder absorption rates, resulting in deficiencies that can affect not just physical health but also mental well-being. Nutrients such as B vitamins, which are crucial for energy production and brain health, may be inadequately absorbed, leading to fatigue and cognitive decline.

The connection between hydration, gut health, and mental health cannot be overstated. The gut-brain axis illustrates how gastrointestinal health impacts mood and cognitive function. Dehydration can lead to increased levels of stress and anxiety, potentially due to the adverse effects on gut microbiota and nutrient absorption. Maintaining proper hydration supports not only gut function but also mental clarity and emotional stability. Thus, prioritizing water intake is essential for anyone looking to enhance their overall health and well-being, emphasizing the integral link between hydration, gut function, and mental health.

The Connection Between Hydration and Cognitive Performance

Hydration plays a critical role in maintaining cognitive performance, significantly influencing various mental processes such as attention, memory, and mood. The human brain, which comprises approximately 75% water, relies on adequate hydration to function optimally. Even mild dehydration, defined as a loss of about 1-2% of body weight due to fluid loss, can lead to noticeable impairments in cognitive abilities. Studies have shown that individuals who are dehydrated often experience difficulties in concentrating, reduced short-term memory, and an increased perception of fatigue. This underscores the importance of maintaining appropriate hydration levels for optimal brain health.

The mechanisms through which hydration affects cognitive function are multifaceted. Water is essential for the transportation of nutrients and oxygen to the brain, facilitating the energy metabolism required for cognitive tasks. Dehydration can lead to increased blood viscosity, which impairs circulation and, consequently, the delivery of essential nutrients to brain cells. Additionally, hydration influences neurotransmitter synthesis and release, which are vital for effective communication between neurons. As a result, even slight changes in hydration status can disrupt these processes and lead to cognitive decline.

Hydration status has been linked to mood regulation, which is an essential component of cognitive performance. Research indicates that dehydration can increase feelings of anxiety and tension while decreasing overall mood. These emotional changes can further impact cognitive functions such as decision-making and problem-solving, creating a feedback loop that exacerbates mental fatigue. Maintaining proper hydration not only supports cognitive functions but also contributes to emotional stability, which is crucial for optimal performance in daily activities and professional tasks.

The sources of hydration are equally important, as not all fluids contribute equally to cognitive health. While water remains the best choice for hydration, certain beverages and foods can also aid in maintaining fluid balance. For instance, fruits and vegetables with high water content, such as cucumbers, oranges, and watermelon, provide essential hydration along with vitamins and minerals. However, beverages high in sugar or caffeine may lead to dehydration in the long term, despite initial feelings of hydration. It is essential to choose hydrating sources wisely to ensure that cognitive functions are not compromised.

The connection between hydration and cognitive performance is clear and significant. Adequate fluid intake is vital for maintaining not only physical health but also mental acuity. Adults should prioritize hydration as a key aspect of their overall health regimen, particularly in a world where cognitive demands are continually increasing. By understanding the importance of hydration and making conscious choices about fluid intake, individuals can support their cognitive functions and enhance their overall quality of life.

Tips for Staying Hydrated

Staying hydrated is essential for overall health, and it plays a significant role in maintaining optimal gut and brain function. The human body is composed of approximately 60% water, and this fluid is crucial for various physiological processes, including digestion, nutrient absorption, and the regulation of body temperature. Dehydration can lead to fatigue, headaches, and impaired cognitive function, highlighting the importance of adequate fluid intake for both physical and mental well-being. Adults should aim to drink enough water throughout the day to support their health and enhance their gut-brain connection.

One effective strategy for ensuring proper hydration is to establish a routine that incorporates water intake into daily activities. For instance, consider drinking a glass of water first thing in the morning to kickstart hydration after a night of sleep. Carrying a reusable water bottle can also serve as a constant reminder to drink water throughout the day. Setting specific goals, such as drinking a certain number of glasses by midday, can help individuals stay accountable and make hydration a priority. By integrating these habits into daily life, individuals can more easily meet their hydration needs.

In addition to water, incorporating hydrating foods into your diet can significantly contribute to overall fluid intake. Fruits and vegetables are excellent sources of hydration due to their high water content. For example, cucumbers, watermelon, and oranges not only provide hydration but also deliver essential vitamins and minerals that support gut health. Including a variety of these foods in your meals and snacks can enhance hydration while simultaneously promoting nutrient diversity, which is crucial for a healthy gut microbiome and optimal brain function.

Monitoring your body's signals can also help manage hydration levels effectively. Thirst is a natural indicator that your body requires fluids, but it's essential to pay attention to other signs as well. Dry mouth, fatigue, and decreased urine output can signal dehydration. To prevent these issues, individuals should drink water regularly, even when they do not feel thirsty. Additionally, paying attention to the color of urine can be a helpful gauge; pale yellow typically indicates adequate hydration, while darker urine may suggest the need for increased fluid intake.

It is important to consider individual factors that may influence hydration needs, such as physical activity, climate, and overall health status. People who engage in strenuous exercise or live in hot environments may require additional fluids to compensate for losses through sweat. Furthermore, certain health conditions and medications can affect hydration levels. Consulting with a healthcare professional can provide personalized recommendations for fluid intake based on specific circumstances. By adopting these tips for staying hydrated, individuals can enhance their gut-brain connection, ultimately supporting their mental health and overall well-being.

Chapter 9: Practical Steps to Improve Gut-Brain Health

Creating a Balanced Diet

Creating a balanced diet is essential for maintaining optimal mental and physical health. A balanced diet provides the necessary nutrients that support brain function, emotional well-being, and overall vitality. To achieve this balance, it is crucial to incorporate a variety of food groups into daily meals, ensuring that the body receives a wide range of vitamins, minerals, and other nutrients that promote gut health and, in turn, enhance mental health.

The foundation of a balanced diet consists of fruits and vegetables, whole grains, lean proteins, and healthy fats. Fruits and vegetables are rich in antioxidants, vitamins, and fiber, which play a significant role in reducing inflammation and supporting gut microbiota diversity. Whole grains, such as brown rice, quinoa, and whole-wheat products, provide essential carbohydrates that fuel the brain and body. Lean proteins, including fish, poultry, legumes, and plant-based sources, are vital for neurotransmitter production, which directly influences mood and cognitive function. Healthy fats, especially those from sources like avocados, nuts, seeds, and olive oil, are important for brain health and can help regulate emotions.

It is also important to consider portion sizes and meal frequency when creating a balanced diet. Eating smaller, more frequent meals can help stabilize blood sugar levels, preventing energy crashes that may lead to irritability and mood swings. Additionally, mindful eating practices encourage individuals to pay attention to hunger cues and make conscious food choices, fostering a healthier relationship with food. This approach can also enhance the enjoyment of meals and contribute to greater satisfaction, further supporting mental well-being.

Incorporating fermented foods into the diet can significantly enhance gut health, which is closely linked to mental health. Foods such as yogurt, kefir, sauerkraut, and kimchi contain probiotics that promote a healthy gut microbiome. A balanced diet rich in these foods can improve digestion, reduce symptoms of anxiety and depression, and enhance overall mental clarity. The gut-brain axis underscores the importance of maintaining a healthy gut to support emotional health, making fermented foods a vital component of a balanced diet.

Hydration plays a crucial yet often overlooked role in maintaining a balanced diet. Adequate water intake is necessary for optimal brain function and mood regulation. Dehydration can lead to fatigue, irritability, and difficulty concentrating, negatively impacting mental health. Therefore, adults should aim to drink sufficient water throughout the day while also considering hydration from food sources such as fruits and vegetables. By focusing on a balanced diet that includes diverse food groups, appropriate portion sizes, fermented foods, and proper hydration, individuals can significantly enhance their gut health and, consequently, their mental well-being.

Incorporating Mindful Eating Practices

Mindful eating is a powerful practice that can significantly enhance our relationship with food and improve both our gut health and mental well-being. This approach encourages individuals to focus on the sensory experience of eating, which includes paying attention to the taste, texture, and aroma of food. By becoming more aware of these sensations, individuals can cultivate a deeper appreciation for their meals, leading to more satisfying and fulfilling eating experiences. This heightened awareness can help prevent overeating, as individuals learn to recognize their hunger and satiety cues more effectively.

To incorporate mindful eating practices, it is essential to create a conducive environment for meals. This means minimizing distractions such as television, smartphones, or other electronic devices. By setting the table and creating a pleasant atmosphere, individuals can signal to their brains that it is time to focus on the act of eating. Additionally, taking a moment to breathe deeply before a meal can help ground individuals in the present moment, allowing them to approach their food with a clear mind and open heart.

Another key aspect of mindful eating is to practice gratitude for the food consumed. Reflecting on the origins of the meal, acknowledging the effort that went into its preparation, and appreciating the nutritional benefits it provides can foster a positive mindset. This practice not only enhances the eating experience but also reinforces the connection between food and well-being. When individuals express gratitude, they are more likely to form a healthier relationship with food, viewing it as nourishment rather than a source of stress or guilt.

Engaging in mindful eating also involves slowing down the pace of eating. Taking smaller bites, chewing thoroughly, and putting down utensils between bites encourages a more deliberate approach to meals. This slower pace allows the brain to register fullness, reducing the likelihood of overeating. Furthermore, savoring each bite can enhance the enjoyment of food, transforming meals into a pleasurable and satisfying experience rather than a rushed obligation.

It is beneficial to reflect on emotional triggers related to eating. Many individuals may find themselves eating out of boredom, stress, or sadness rather than genuine hunger. By identifying these emotional patterns, individuals can work towards more mindful choices, opting for healthier coping mechanisms such as physical activity, journaling, or meditation. This awareness not only supports better eating habits but also promotes overall mental health, creating a harmonious balance between the gut and the brain.

Building a Sustainable Nutrition Plan

Building a sustainable nutrition plan is essential for maintaining both physical health and mental well-being. A sustainable nutrition plan is one that is practical, adaptable, and focuses on long-term health benefits rather than quick fixes. To create such a plan, individuals should first assess their current dietary habits and identify areas for improvement. This process often involves tracking food intake, understanding individual nutritional needs, and recognizing emotional eating triggers. By gaining insight into personal eating patterns, individuals can make informed decisions that align with their health goals.

Next, incorporating a variety of whole foods into the diet is crucial for fostering a sustainable nutrition plan. Whole foods, such as fruits, vegetables, whole grains, lean proteins, and healthy fats, provide essential nutrients that support both gut and brain health. These foods are rich in vitamins, minerals, antioxidants, and fiber, which play significant roles in reducing inflammation and promoting a healthy microbiome. Moreover, a diverse diet helps to ensure that individuals receive a broad spectrum of nutrients, which can positively influence mood and cognitive function, fostering a connection between nutrition and mental health.

Meal planning and preparation can significantly enhance the sustainability of a nutrition plan. By dedicating time each week to plan meals, individuals can make conscious choices about what they eat, reducing reliance on processed foods and impulsive eating. Preparing meals in advance not only saves time during busy weekdays but also encourages healthier choices. Incorporating batch cooking, utilizing seasonal ingredients, and experimenting with new recipes can keep the meal plan exciting and aligned with nutritional goals. Additionally, this practice can help manage portion sizes and minimize food waste, contributing to overall sustainability.

Mindful eating practices are another essential component of a sustainable nutrition plan. This approach encourages individuals to pay attention to their hunger and fullness cues, promoting a healthier relationship with food. Mindful eating can help reduce emotional eating and promote a more satisfying dining experience, ultimately leading to better food choices. By slowing down during meals and savoring each bite, individuals can enhance their awareness of food quality and its impact on both gut health and mental well-being, reinforcing the gut-brain connection.

Flexibility is vital to maintaining a sustainable nutrition plan. A rigid diet can lead to feelings of deprivation and frustration, making it challenging to stick to long-term. Instead, individuals should allow for occasional indulgences and variations in their diet. This flexibility helps to cultivate a balanced approach to nutrition, ensuring that healthy eating remains enjoyable rather than a chore. By focusing on overall patterns rather than perfection, individuals can create a sustainable nutrition plan that supports their health and mental well-being for years to come.

Chapter 10: Case Studies and Real-Life Applications

Success Stories of Dietary Changes

In recent years, numerous studies have highlighted the profound impact of dietary changes on mental health, with many individuals experiencing significant improvements in their emotional well-being. One compelling success story is that of Sarah, a 34-year-old woman who struggled with anxiety and depression for over a decade. After consulting with a nutritionist, she decided to eliminate processed foods and increase her intake of whole, nutrient-dense foods. Within months, Sarah reported a marked reduction in her anxiety levels. Her daily mood swings diminished, and she found herself able to engage more fully in activities that once felt overwhelming. Sarah's journey emphasizes the potential of dietary adjustments to facilitate mental health recovery.

Similarly, Tom, a 45-year-old man diagnosed with ADHD, underwent a dietary overhaul that transformed his daily life. After researching the gut-brain connection, he learned about the benefits of omega-3 fatty acids, probiotics, and a balanced diet rich in fruits and vegetables. By incorporating fish, nuts, and fermented foods into his meals, Tom experienced improved focus and reduced impulsivity. His work performance improved, and he found it easier to maintain healthy relationships. Tom's case illustrates that targeted dietary interventions can lead to significant behavioral changes, highlighting the importance of nutrition in managing ADHD symptoms.

Another inspiring story comes from Emily, a college student who faced severe mood swings and fatigue due to her unhealthy eating habits. Upon realizing that her diet primarily consisted of sugary snacks and caffeine, she decided to make a change. Emily began meal prepping, focusing on whole grains, leafy greens, and lean proteins. She also cut back on sugar and caffeine, opting for herbal teas instead. As her diet improved, so did her energy levels and emotional stability. Emily's experience serves as a testament to the power of mindful eating and its capacity to enhance overall mental health.

The success stories of dietary changes are not limited to individuals; families also experience transformative benefits. The Martinez family, for instance, struggled with various health issues, including obesity and mood disorders. By collectively adopting a plant-based diet, they not only improved their physical health but also fostered a supportive family environment. Meal planning and cooking together became a bonding experience, reducing stress and promoting healthier eating habits for all family members. Their story illustrates how dietary changes can create a ripple effect, positively influencing not just mental health but familial relationships.

The case of David, a retired veteran suffering from PTSD, emphasizes the role of nutrition in recovery. After years of relying on medication, David sought alternative therapies and learned about the impact of gut health on mental wellness. By incorporating a diet rich in antioxidants and anti-inflammatory foods, such as berries, nuts, and leafy greens, he noticed a significant decrease in his symptoms. David's experience underscores the potential for dietary changes to complement traditional therapeutic approaches, promoting a holistic path to mental health recovery. These success stories collectively highlight the vital connection between nutrition and mental well-being, encouraging others to explore dietary changes as a means of enhancing their own mental health.

Professional Insights from Nutritionists

Nutritionists play a crucial role in understanding the intricate relationship between diet and mental health, particularly how the foods we consume can influence our gut microbiome and, subsequently, our emotional well-being. Their expertise provides valuable insights into how specific nutrients affect brain function, mood regulation, and cognitive performance. By examining current research and clinical practices, nutritionists shed light on the importance of a balanced diet tailored to support both physical and mental health.

One of the primary areas of focus for nutritionists is the impact of gut health on mental health. The gut microbiome, which comprises trillions of microorganisms, plays a significant role in producing neurotransmitters such as serotonin and dopamine, which are essential for mood stabilization. Nutritionists emphasize the importance of incorporating foods rich in prebiotics and probiotics, such as fermented foods and fiber-rich fruits and vegetables, to promote a healthy gut environment. This understanding helps to create dietary recommendations that not only enhance digestive health but also support emotional balance.

Nutritionists also highlight the significance of omega-3 fatty acids in mental health. These essential fats, found in fatty fish, walnuts, and flaxseeds, are known for their anti-inflammatory properties and their role in brain structure and function. Research suggests that adequate intake of omega-3s can reduce symptoms of depression and anxiety, making them an essential component of any diet aimed at improving mental health. By educating clients on the benefits of these nutrients, nutritionists can guide them toward making informed dietary choices that align with their mental health goals.

The relationship between sugar intake and mental health is a critical area of exploration for nutritionists. High sugar consumption has been linked to increased risk of mood disorders, as it can lead to blood sugar spikes and crashes, resulting in irritability and fatigue. Nutritionists advocate for a balanced approach to carbohydrates, encouraging the consumption of whole grains and complex carbohydrates that provide sustained energy and support overall mental clarity. This focus on mindful eating habits empowers individuals to make choices that positively impact their mood and cognitive function.

Nutritionists stress the importance of a holistic approach to dietary changes. They encourage clients to consider not just what they eat, but how they eat. Mindful eating practices, such as paying attention to hunger cues and appreciating the sensory experience of food, can enhance the overall impact of nutrition on mental health. By integrating these practices into daily routines, individuals can foster a healthier relationship with food, ultimately contributing to improved emotional well-being. Through their professional insights, nutritionists play an essential role in bridging the gap between nutrition and mental health, providing adults with the tools they need to cultivate better emotional resilience through diet.

Lessons Learned from Research

Research on the gut-brain connection has illuminated several key lessons that emphasize the intricate relationship between nutrition and mental health. One of the most significant findings is the role of the gut microbiome in influencing brain function. The gut houses trillions of microorganisms, which not only aid in digestion but also produce neurotransmitters and other compounds that can affect mood and cognitive abilities. This discovery underscores the importance of maintaining a balanced diet rich in prebiotics and probiotics to support a healthy microbiome, thereby promoting optimal mental health.

Another critical lesson from the research is the impact of inflammation on both gut health and mental well-being. Chronic inflammation has been linked to various mental health disorders, including depression and anxiety. Studies have shown that a diet high in processed foods, sugar, and unhealthy fats can exacerbate inflammation, while a diet rich in whole foods, omega-3 fatty acids, and antioxidants can help mitigate it. This finding highlights the need for individuals to be mindful of their dietary choices, as these can either contribute to or alleviate inflammatory responses in the body.

The research has revealed the importance of specific nutrients in supporting mental health. For example, deficiencies in vitamins such as B12, D, and omega-3 fatty acids have been associated with mood disorders. Incorporating foods rich in these essential nutrients can provide significant benefits for mental health. This lesson emphasizes the necessity of a well-rounded diet that includes a variety of nutrient-dense foods to ensure that the body, and by extension the brain, receives the necessary building blocks for optimal function.

The connection between gut health and mental health also extends to the concept of the gut-brain axis, which refers to the bidirectional communication between the gut and the brain. Research has demonstrated that stress can alter gut permeability, leading to conditions like leaky gut syndrome, which can, in turn, affect mental health. This bi-directional relationship suggests that managing stress through mindfulness practices, exercise, and adequate sleep can have a profound impact on gut health and, ultimately, mental well-being.

Findings from research emphasize the need for a holistic approach to mental health that integrates dietary choices with other lifestyle factors. Nutrition alone is not a panacea; it must be combined with physical activity, social connections, and mental health awareness to promote overall well-being. The lessons learned from the research highlight the importance of viewing mental health through a comprehensive lens, recognizing that the interplay between diet, lifestyle, and mental health is complex but essential for achieving a balanced and healthy life.

Chapter 11: Future Directions in Gut-Brain Research

Emerging Trends in Nutrition Science

Emerging trends in nutrition science are rapidly reshaping our understanding of the gut-brain connection and its implications for mental health. As research continues to unveil the intricate relationship between diet and psychological well-being, several key themes are gaining prominence. These trends highlight the importance of personalized nutrition, the role of the microbiome, and the impact of food quality on mental health. By examining these areas, we can better appreciate how our dietary choices influence not only physical health but also emotional and cognitive function.

Personalized nutrition is at the forefront of emerging trends, emphasizing the need for tailored dietary recommendations based on individual biology. Advances in genomics and metabolomics are enabling researchers to identify how different people respond to various nutrients and foods. This approach moves away from the one-size-fits-all model, acknowledging that factors such as genetics, lifestyle, and microbiome composition can significantly influence nutritional needs. As a result, personalized nutrition holds promise for enhancing mental health outcomes by optimizing dietary interventions according to an individual's unique profile.

Another critical trend is the growing recognition of the gut microbiome's role in mental health. The trillions of microorganisms residing in our digestive tract can affect brain function through several mechanisms, including the production of neurotransmitters, modulation of inflammation, and influence on gut-brain signaling pathways. Research is increasingly demonstrating that a diverse and balanced microbiome is associated with improved mood and cognitive function. Consequently, strategies that promote microbiome health, such as prebiotics, probiotics, and a diet rich in fiber, are gaining traction in the field of nutrition science as potential interventions for mental health issues.

The quality of food consumed is also receiving heightened attention in discussions about nutrition and mental health. Diets high in processed foods, sugars, and unhealthy fats have been linked to an increased risk of mood disorders and cognitive decline. Conversely, whole foods, including fruits, vegetables, whole grains, lean proteins, and healthy fats, are associated with better mental health outcomes. This trend emphasizes the importance of not just what we eat, but how food quality can influence our psychological well-being. Encouraging a shift towards whole, nutrient-dense foods may help mitigate the prevalence of mental health disorders in the population.

Integration of nutritional psychiatry into clinical practice is an emerging trend that underscores the importance of diet in treating mental health conditions. Mental health professionals are increasingly recognizing the value of dietary interventions as complementary treatments alongside traditional therapies. This multidisciplinary approach fosters collaboration between dietitians and mental health practitioners, ensuring that patients receive comprehensive care that addresses both their physical and psychological needs. As the field continues to evolve, the incorporation of nutrition science into mental health care is likely to become a standard practice, ultimately enhancing patient outcomes and promoting overall well-being.

The Role of Technology in Gut Health

The role of technology in gut health has become increasingly significant as researchers and health professionals seek to understand the complex interactions between diet, gut microbiota, and mental well-being. Advanced technologies such as DNA sequencing and microbiome analysis have revolutionized our ability to study the gut microbiome, allowing for greater insights into how specific bacteria influence health outcomes. These tools enable scientists to identify which microbial species are beneficial, harmful, or neutral, thus providing a clearer picture of how individual variations in gut flora can affect mental health.

Wearable devices and mobile health applications are also playing a critical role in monitoring gut health. These technologies can track dietary intake, physical activity, sleep patterns, and stress levels, all of which are vital components of gut health. By collecting and analyzing this data, individuals can gain insights into their personal health behaviors and make more informed choices. Some applications even provide personalized dietary recommendations based on the user's specific gut microbiome profile, thereby facilitating tailored nutrition plans that can enhance both gut and mental health.

Telemedicine has further expanded access to gut health services, allowing individuals to consult with nutritionists and gastroenterologists without the barriers of location or time constraints. This has proven especially beneficial for those who may not have access to specialized care in their area. Through virtual consultations, health professionals can guide patients on how to optimize their diets and lifestyles to support gut health, which in turn can lead to improved mental health outcomes. The convenience of telemedicine encourages more individuals to seek help, ultimately fostering a proactive approach to gut health.

Artificial intelligence and machine learning are also beginning to play a role in understanding the gut-brain connection. These technologies can analyze vast amounts of data from various sources, such as clinical studies, health records, and dietary surveys, to identify patterns and correlations that may not be evident to human researchers. By predicting how certain dietary changes might impact gut microbiota and, consequently, mental health, AI can assist in developing more effective interventions tailored to individual needs.

Technology is reshaping our understanding of gut health and its implications for mental well-being. From advanced microbiome analysis to mobile health applications and telemedicine, the integration of technology into health practices offers new avenues for improving gut health. As research continues to evolve, these innovations will likely lead to more personalized and effective strategies for maintaining a healthy gut, which is essential for overall mental health.

Potential Therapies and Interventions

The exploration of potential therapies and interventions for enhancing mental health through nutrition is a rapidly evolving field, rooted in the emerging understanding of the gut-brain connection. Research indicates that the gut microbiome plays a significant role in regulating mood and cognitive functions, which has led to a growing interest in nutritional interventions aimed at optimizing gut health. These interventions can range from dietary modifications to the use of specific supplements, and they hold promise for individuals seeking to improve their mental well-being through natural means.

One of the most straightforward approaches to improving gut health is through dietary changes. A diet rich in fiber, fruits, vegetables, whole grains, and fermented foods can promote the growth of beneficial gut bacteria. Foods such as yogurt, kefir, sauerkraut, and kimchi introduce probiotics, which are live microorganisms that confer health benefits. These dietary adjustments can not only enhance gut microbiota diversity but also lead to improved production of neurotransmitters, such as serotonin, which is crucial for mood regulation.

In addition to dietary modifications, supplementation can serve as an effective intervention. Probiotic supplements specifically designed to target mental health issues have gained attention. Certain strains of probiotics have shown promise in clinical studies for reducing anxiety and depressive symptoms. Omega-3 fatty acids, commonly found in fish oil, are another supplement linked to brain health. They have anti-inflammatory properties and are associated with improved mood and cognitive function. The therapeutic potential of these supplements underscores the importance of a holistic approach to mental health, integrating dietary and supplementary strategies.

Mindfulness and stress-reduction techniques also play a vital role in the gut-brain connection. Chronic stress can negatively impact gut health, leading to dysbiosis, which may result in further mental health issues. Interventions such as mindfulness meditation, yoga, and cognitive-behavioral therapy can help manage stress levels and, by extension, support gut health. These practices not only foster a sense of well-being but also create a favorable environment for beneficial gut bacteria to thrive, thereby enhancing the gut-brain communication pathways.

Personalized nutrition is emerging as a key strategy in the field of mental health interventions. Understanding that each individual's gut microbiome is unique allows for tailored dietary recommendations that cater to specific needs. This personalized approach can optimize the effectiveness of nutritional therapies, ensuring that interventions are more targeted and beneficial. As research continues to uncover the complexities of the gut-brain connection, it is essential for individuals to consider these potential therapies and interventions as part of a comprehensive strategy for enhancing mental health and overall well-being.

Chapter 12: Conclusion and Takeaways

Summary of Key Concepts

The gut-brain connection is a complex and dynamic relationship that underscores the interplay between our gastrointestinal system and mental health. This connection is primarily facilitated by the vagus nerve, which serves as a communication pathway between the gut and the brain. Through this neural network, the brain receives signals about the state of the gut, which can influence mood, cognition, and overall mental well-being. Understanding this connection is crucial for recognizing how dietary choices can impact mental health, emphasizing the importance of a balanced diet rich in nutrients that support both physical and emotional health.

One of the key concepts within this subchapter is the role of the microbiome, the community of microorganisms residing in the gut. Research indicates that the microbiome plays a vital role in producing neurotransmitters such as serotonin, which is often referred to as the "feel-good" hormone. Approximately 90% of the body's serotonin is produced in the gut, highlighting the significance of gut health in regulating mood and emotional states. A diverse and balanced microbiome is essential for optimal neurotransmitter production, pointing to the importance of dietary fibers, probiotics, and prebiotics in maintaining a healthy gut environment.

The concept of inflammation is critical in understanding the gut-brain connection. Chronic inflammation in the body can lead to various health issues, including mental health disorders such as anxiety and depression. Diets high in processed foods and sugars can promote inflammation, while anti-inflammatory foods like fatty fish, nuts, and leafy greens can help mitigate these effects.

By focusing on anti-inflammatory nutrition, individuals can potentially reduce the risk of developing mental health issues linked to inflammation, reinforcing the idea that what we eat directly affects our emotional health.

Another vital aspect of this connection is the influence of stress on gut health. Stress can negatively impact the gut microbiome, leading to dysbiosis, which can in turn affect mental health. Stressful situations often lead to poor dietary choices, such as increased consumption of comfort foods high in sugar and fat, further exacerbating the gut-brain relationship. Learning stress management techniques and adopting a nutrient-dense diet can help break this cycle, promoting both gut and mental health.

The integration of nutritional psychology into the understanding of the gut-brain connection emphasizes the psychological aspects of eating behavior. This field examines how thoughts, feelings, and behaviors influence our food choices and, consequently, our gut health. By fostering a positive relationship with food, individuals can make more informed dietary choices that not only nourish their bodies but also support their mental health. Awareness of the gut-brain connection can empower adults to take charge of their health through mindful eating practices, ultimately leading to improved emotional and psychological well-being.

Steps for Ongoing Improvement

Ongoing improvement in understanding the gut-brain connection requires a commitment to continuous learning and adaptation of nutritional strategies. The first step in this process is to cultivate a mindset of curiosity and openness towards new research findings and dietary approaches. Adults should actively seek out credible sources of information, such as scientific journals, nutrition workshops, and seminars led by experts. Engaging in discussions with healthcare professionals can also provide insights into the latest advancements in nutrition and mental health. This proactive approach to learning helps individuals make informed decisions about their dietary choices and encourages a deeper understanding of how these choices impact overall well-being.

Another crucial step is to regularly assess and monitor personal dietary habits and mental health. Keeping a food diary can be a powerful tool for identifying patterns and triggers related to both physical and mental health. By documenting food intake, mood changes, and energy levels, individuals can gain valuable insights into how specific foods affect their mental state. This practice not only promotes mindfulness regarding food choices but also allows for adjustments to be made based on personal experiences. Regular self-assessment creates a feedback loop that fosters ongoing improvement and encourages individuals to experiment with different foods and dietary strategies.

Incorporating a variety of nutrient-dense foods into one's diet is essential for ongoing improvement. A diverse diet rich in fruits, vegetables, whole grains, lean proteins, and healthy fats supports gut health and, consequently, mental health. Foods that are high in fiber, such as legumes and whole grains, promote a healthy microbiome, which has been linked to improved mood and cognitive function. Additionally, the inclusion of fermented foods like yogurt, sauerkraut, and kimchi can enhance gut health by introducing beneficial probiotics. Adults should prioritize exploring new recipes and food combinations that emphasize these nutrient-rich ingredients, which can lead to both enjoyment and health benefits.

Creating a supportive environment is another key factor in fostering ongoing improvement. This includes surrounding oneself with like-minded individuals who prioritize health and well-being. Joining community groups or online forums focused on nutrition and mental health can provide encouragement and motivation. Sharing experiences and strategies with others can also lead to the discovery of new ideas and approaches that facilitate personal growth. Furthermore, developing a routine that incorporates regular meal planning and preparation can reduce the likelihood of reverting to unhealthy eating habits during times of stress or busyness.

It is important to acknowledge that ongoing improvement is a journey rather than a destination. While it is beneficial to set specific health and nutrition goals, flexibility and patience are essential. Life circumstances may change, and what works at one point may need to be adjusted later on. Adults should embrace this process by celebrating small successes and learning from setbacks. By maintaining a long-term perspective and being willing to adapt, individuals can cultivate a healthier relationship with food and enhance their mental health over time. This approach ensures that the gut-brain connection continues to be a central focus in their lives, leading to sustained well-being and resilience.

The Future of Gut-Brain Health Awareness

The future of gut-brain health awareness is poised to evolve significantly as research continues to uncover the intricate connections between our gut microbiome and mental health. As more studies highlight the impact of nutrition on cognitive function and emotional well-being, there is an increasing recognition among health professionals and the public alike of the importance of gut health. This shift is likely to foster a greater emphasis on preventive care, encouraging individuals to adopt dietary practices that support both their physical and mental health.

In upcoming years, we can expect advancements in personalized nutrition based on individual microbiome profiles. As technology continues to develop, it will become more feasible for healthcare providers to offer tailored dietary recommendations that promote gut health and, by extension, mental health. The integration of microbiome analysis into routine health assessments will empower individuals to make informed choices about their diets, leading to improved overall well-being. This personalized approach will help bridge the gap between traditional healthcare practices and the burgeoning field of nutritional psychiatry.

In tandem with personalized nutrition, educational initiatives will play a crucial role in raising awareness about the gut-brain connection. Public health campaigns and community programs will likely emerge, aimed at informing adults about the significance of gut health for mental clarity and emotional resilience. As knowledge dissemination becomes more widespread, individuals will be better equipped to make dietary choices that align with their health goals, fostering a culture of proactive health management. This educational focus will be essential in debunking myths and misconceptions surrounding nutrition and mental health.

The future will also see an increase in collaborative efforts among researchers, healthcare providers, and nutritionists to create evidence-based guidelines for maintaining gut health. These guidelines will likely synthesize findings from a variety of disciplines, including gastroenterology, psychology, and nutrition science. By working together, professionals can develop comprehensive strategies that address both the physiological and psychological aspects of gut health. Such collaboration will facilitate a holistic approach to wellness, recognizing the interdependence of physical and mental health.

As the conversation around gut-brain health continues to expand, it is anticipated that policymakers will take notice and support initiatives that promote research and education in this area. Funding for studies exploring the gut microbiome's influence on mental health will likely increase, paving the way for groundbreaking discoveries. Additionally, policies that encourage access to nutrient-rich foods and support for mental health resources will be essential in creating an environment where gut-brain health is prioritized. As awareness grows, the hope is that society will move towards a more integrated understanding of health, where nutrition is seen not just as a means of sustenance but as a critical component of mental well-being.